Story Link® Program

JESUS
AND
THE VERY BEST BIRTHDAY
by Sunny Griffin

Illustrated by Andra Chase

DID YOU KNOW...
Mary rode a donkey
when she and Joseph
went to Bethlehem to
pay their taxes?

DID YOU KNOW...
The city was crowded,
the inn was full, and
Mary and Joseph had
no place to stay?

DID YOU KNOW...
The innkeeper told Mary and Joseph they could sleep in his stable with the animals?

DID YOU KNOW...
Jesus was born in that stable on a cold winter night a long time ago?

DID YOU KNOW...
On that special night
a big shiny star
appeared high in the
sky?

DID YOU KNOW...
Mary wrapped baby
Jesus in soft warm
cloths and laid him in
a manger-bed filled
with sweet-smelling
hay?

DID YOU KNOW...
The animals in the stable were very quiet so baby Jesus could sleep?

DID YOU KNOW...
Joseph watched over
baby Jesus and Mary
as they rested?

DID YOU KNOW...
Shepherds watching their sheep out in the fields heard about Jesus from an angel?

DID YOU KNOW...
The shepherds hurried into the city and found baby Jesus lying in the manger, just as the angel had said?

DID YOU KNOW...
Wise men from a faraway land followed the big shiny star when they came to see Jesus?

DID YOU KNOW...
Jesus' birth was the very best birthday ever?

Because God gave his only Son, Jesus, as a special gift to all of us!